G000123147

By

Louise Humphrey
James Bradley
Amy Somers
Guy Gilpin

Thanks to Mother Tongue's
copywriters around the world
for their contributions.

Published in 2011 by Mother Tongue Ltd.,
21 Heathmans Road, London SW6 4TJ,
United Kingdom. www.mothertongue.com

The paper used is a natural, recyclable
product made from wood grown in
sustainable forests. Printed in Denmark.

ISBN 978-0-9568924-0-9

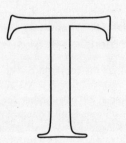

What is transcreation?

Effectively translating marketing material and other creative texts, such as books and screenplays, is a tricky business. It's about much more than converting words from one language to another — it's about ensuring that all the different elements that make up a text (the style, tone, idioms and analogies to name just a few) are accurately tailored to the target audience.

In short, the finished text should read as if it were originally written in the reader's own mother tongue, and give them the exact same experience as the source text gave to readers in the original language.

This process is far more complex than translation – it is what we call transcreation.

Someone who can transcreate copy must have a sound knowledge of the source language, and be a mother tongue speaker of the target language. They must have an in-depth understanding of the two cultures involved, and be an accomplished writer. This gives them the confidence to move away from the original text when necessary, without changing words and ideas simply for the sake of change.

About this book

This book is bursting with all kinds of thought-provoking insights into the creative translation process.

It contains examples of successfully transcreated campaigns, embarrassing blunders, cultural faux pas and pitfalls to look out for, interesting quotes, tips and tricks – and everything in-between.

Dip into the book at random
for inspiration and guidance.

Whatever your profession,
we're sure you'll find
something of interest. We hope
you have as much fun reading
it as we did writing it.

Translation is about the ability to understand someone else's language.

Transcreation is about the
ability to write in your own.

It's not just English brands that often leave slogans in the original language for international audiences.

Car maker Volkswagen is using its "Das Auto" line worldwide. It highlights the fact that the cars come from Germany – a country known for high-quality engineering.

But in Brazil the strategy has backfired.

The VW Beetle was made there for decades, and the brand was seen as an "honorary Brazilian". This was reflected in its previous slogan, "você conhece, você confia" ("you know, you trust"). By emphasizing its foreign-ness, VW threw away an emotional bond built up over many years.

By contrast, the German line was well received in Russia. Market research is crucial!

Transcreation takes into account the difference in contexts between the source and target versions. This often means making cultural adjustments.

In the biblical phrase "The Lamb of God", the lamb symbolizes innocence.

But in the Inuit (Eskimo) version of the Bible, this expression is translated as "The Seal of God".

This is because seals represent innocence in Eskimo culture.

After all, you don't find many lambs running around on the Arctic ice cap …

When McDonald's decided to adapt its iconic "i'm lovin' it!" tagline for the Chinese market, it opted against literal translation. This is because the word "love" in China is taken very seriously and never used lightly. Traditionally, the word "love" was never even said aloud. Even today, lovers say, "I like you" to communicate great affection without actually using the word.

As a result, McDonald's opted
for this Mandarin line:

我就喜欢

This literally means "I just
like (it)".

This is more normal, everyday
vocab, and is easier on the
ears for a Chinese audience.
The line also retains the same
youthful, confident street
vibe of the English.

Often, companies who go for the cheap option of translating something poorly without showing any cultural sensitivity end up having to redo the work.

This happened to the US Warner Channel, who used non-native translators and voice talent to produce all of the Portuguese content for the Brazil version of their channel.

The mistake-ridden subtitles and US-accented Portuguese voice-overs soon became a national joke.

After countless complaints about the lack of respect for the Brazilian audience, Warner finally hired local professionals.

Luxury French hotel brand Sofitel took a novel approach to creating a signature for use on the French and English versions of its website. Instead of creating one in English, and then having it transcreated into French, or vice-versa, they came up with "Life is Magnifique".

The dual-language line works in both France and the UK, as the word "magnifique" sounds similar enough to the English word "magnificent" for it to be understood by the English audience, while the word "life" is easy for French people to understand. Yet at the same time, the overall line has a certain feel of French elegance.

When Chinese shops first imported Coca-Cola in the 1920s, they wrote the name in Chinese characters.

Unlike our letters, Chinese characters have both a meaning and a sound.

The characters pronounced "Coca-Cola" often had nonsensical meanings like "mare stuffed with wax" or "bite the wax tadpole".

So for its official Chinese launch in 1928, the brand chose a different name:

可口可樂 (in original traditional form)

The pronunciation was only slightly different ("Kokou-Kolay"), and it meant "a pleasure in the mouth".

It is a transcreation that is almost as successful as the brand behind it.

Differences in writing styles often go well beyond words in different languages.

In English and Northern European languages, there is an emphasis on logical structure. ("Tell them what you're going to tell them, tell them, tell them what you've just told them.")

In languages such as French or Spanish, this style is often thought dull or inelegant.

Digressions are seen as a sign of intellect, not disorganization.

And in Asian languages, people tend to talk around the subject. Concerns about loss of face mean it is common to present all sides of an issue, with conclusions only hinted at, not explicitly stated.

A recent Intel campaign in Brazil shows a great example of effective transcreation. The original English slogan was "Sponsors of Tomorrow". But if translated directly into Portuguese, this would imply that the brand doesn't yet deliver on its promises. The solution was to find something relevant to a country that is becoming more technological and is known for its passion.

The chosen line in Brazil,
"Apaixonados pelo futuro"
("In love with the future"),
fitted the bill perfectly: it's
an emotional line that evokes
desire (as Brazilians are
falling more and more "in
love" with the latest
high-tech products), while
keeping the values of the
rational, original English line.

People may share a language, but be divided by cultural factors that stop communications from working.

For example, Northern Ireland has a strong sectarian divide between Catholics and Protestants that does not exist elsewhere in the UK.

In 1690, Protestant King William of Orange defeated a Catholic army.

Ever since, orange has been a symbol of Protestantism.

Mobile network Orange had great success with the tagline "The future's bright, the future's Orange" on the UK mainland, but this would not have gone down well with the Catholic population in Northern Ireland.

In 2007, Rexona's advertising agency produced a poster. The visual showed a woman's armpit tattooed with an image of a pig.

The UK creatives came up with the line "Don't let body odour brand you!"

The ad was meant to be provocative – but Unilever didn't predict the reaction in Russia.

The translation ("Не дай запаху пота поставить на тебе клеймо!") was straightforward.

But the pig analogy so offended women there that the campaign had to be withdrawn.

Interestingly, the ad was well received in other parts of Eastern Europe, which goes to show how important it is to research the target market.

Even in countries that share a language, words don't always share their meanings.

In Mexico, "cajeta" is a thick, caramel-like spread. Confectionery company Hershey's put this in a chocolate bar, which it called "Cajeta Elegancita".

It was a success, and they started exporting it to the rest of Latin America.

But in Argentina, they hit a problem.

There, "cajeta" is called "dulce de leche" (the name by which it is known in the English-speaking world). "Cajeta" is a word for female genitalia.

A classic case of two countries divided by a common language.

Haribo is to Germans what Cadbury is to the British – an institution. So when they decided to launch their products in the UK, it was important that the tagline was spot-on.

The original German line is "Haribo macht Kinder froh, und Erwachsene ebenso".

A literal translation of this would be "Haribo makes kids happy, and adults too".

While grammatically correct, this English is pretty flat as it lacks the punchy rhythm and rhyme of the original.

And so the following line was born: "Kids and grown-ups love it so, the happy world of Haribo".

A consumer who sees your ad in Berlin or Bangkok doesn't care that it was originally written in English. It is competing for attention with ads that were written in the local language.

A transcreation will compete for this attention on equal terms. A translation almost certainly won't.

It's important to research your product name in the market you want to break into. Even if a certain word doesn't "look" offensive, sometimes the way it is pronounced can give it a whole new meaning.

When Vicks first introduced its cough drops to the German market, they were embarrassed to learn that the Germans pronounce "v" as "f" – and "ficken" is a crude term for "have sex" in German.

In the 90s, a mineral water called "Blue Water" was launched in Russia.

But when Russians said the English name aloud, it sounded very like "блевота" (pronounced "blevOta") – slang for "vomit".

So they changed the name to "Water Blue" – a simple solution, but one that sounds much more appealing.

In 1999, Procter and Gamble launched its new "Swiffer" range of dusting products with the line "When Swiffer's the one, consider it done".

A direct Italian translation wouldn't have had the same impact, not least because it wouldn't have rhymed.
So a transcreation was necessary.

This was "La polvere non dura, perché Swiffer la cattura" ("Dust doesn't linger, because Swiffer catches it").

This actually improves on the original. It not only rhymes, it mentions the benefit ("eliminates dust") and the mechanism of action ("capture"). It is considered among the most effective Italian taglines of recent years.

Brand names too sometimes need transcreation.

The Mitsubishi Pajero SUV was named after the Pampas Cat of Argentina (scientific name: *Leopardus pajeros*).

However, in Spain and Latin America, it is called the Montero (meaning "mountain warrior").

Why? Because "pajero" is a derogatory sexual term in Spanish.

"It were as wise to cast a violet into a crucible that you might discover the formal principle of its colour and odour, as seek to transfuse from one language into another the creations of a poet. The plant must spring again from its seed, or it will bear no flower."

Percy Bysshe Shelley, 1792–1822, on why a brief is important.

Then felt I like some watcher
of the skies
When a new planet swims
into his ken;
Or like stout Cortez when
with eagle eyes
He star'd at the Pacific —
and all his men
Look'd at each other with
a wild surmise —
Silent, upon a peak in Darien.

John Keats, 1795–1821,
on the power of transcreation

"We don't need it done by a copywriter: it was done by a copywriter in English, we just need it translated so it says the same thing."

"How can this tagline cost more than an email? It's only three words."

These are genuine quotes from clients who wanted foreign-language advertising.

What they didn't realize
was that the more creativity
went into the original, the
more creativity it can take to
make it work in other
languages.

Hopefully if they read this
book, they'll realize why.

Sometimes, you have to accept that a concept simply doesn't work in another country or language.

This issue occurred once with the English line "Sense & simplicity" for Philips.

This is impossible to adapt for two reasons.

The book – and therefore the phrase – "Sense and Sensibility" is not known in other countries. Plus, the words for these two ideas are unlikely to be alliterative when translated.

The best thing to do in such a situation is start again from brief. Sadly, in Germany Philips chose just to run the English line – which hardly anyone understood.

"If you talk to a man in a
language he understands,
that goes to his head.
If you talk to him in his
language, that goes to his
heart."

Nelson Mandela

"Translation is like a woman ... If it is beautiful, it is not faithful. If it is faithful, it is most certainly not beautiful."

Yevgeny Yevtushenko

It is a common marketing practice to leave slogans, titles etc. in English.

But just because English is the global language, it doesn't mean people's levels of English are the same around the globe.

Even when a title is not translated, it may still need to be transcreated.

Take the film "Date Night".
The title seems simple enough
– but research found that
French people aren't
familiar with the word "date"
in the sense of a romantic
meeting.

The film was therefore
retitled "Crazy Night".

Whatever the language,
you need to know your
audience.

When De Beers wanted to advertise its diamonds in China in the 1990s, a direct translation of the English line "A diamond is forever" wouldn't have worked in Mandarin. It would have sounded abrupt and confusing, as it would have been understood as "A diamond lasts forever" rather than "A diamond is something to keep forever".

The line was transcreated to "钻石恒久远，一颗永流传", which literally means "Diamond is forever, it will always be handed down (to future generations)". Poetic language is very popular in China, and the line sounded like a quote from a beautiful poem, with an elegant and sophisticated ring to it. The line became an instant hit, and was remembered fondly for years afterwards.

Contrary to what people may think, transcreation is not just relevant to creative copy.

For example, documents relating to recruitment policies and training manuals may not work well when translated literally, as people's motivations and attitudes are so different across cultures.

US training tends to be more interactive and hands-on, whereas people in France tend to prefer more information and less participation.

If this is not reflected when preparing the French materials, they are unlikely to be as effective in France as the originals were in the US.

However good a transcreator is, they can't stay on brief unless they've seen the brief.

And they can't make sure the copy works with the layout unless they've seen the layout.

Give your foreign writers all the same information you'd give to people producing communications in your own language.

It is hard to know what is normal in other cultures.

In World War II, one American spy was caught by the Germans simply because of the way he held his knife and fork while eating.

That whole James Bond thing where the KGB can't tell he's not Russian is entertaining, but implausible.

To blend into another culture, you need someone from that culture to help you.

And that goes for marketing messages as much as international espionage.

A little local knowledge goes a long way.

When a pharmaceutical multinational launched a new product internationally, they thought they could avoid translation issues by using pictures to explain the benefit.

The picture on the left showed an ill patient, the middle picture showed the patient taking the medication, and the picture on the right showed him looking well again.

Among the markets for the launch was the United Arab Emirates.

Arabic speakers read from right to left.

In most markets, Xbox leaves its "Jump in" tagline in English.

However, in France it is a legal requirement that all English used in advertising also has a French version.

A literal translation of the line would be "Saute dedans". While grammatically correct, this does not sound snappy, and does not convey the same sense of getting involved as the English does.

So instead, they opted for the transcreation "Lance-toi".

This literally means "Launch yourself".

It retains the sentiment of the original, and expresses it in a bold, Xbox-like way.

International brands are only too aware of the effect that substandard foreign copy can have on their business:

"In a recent usability study conducted in Germany, Dell observed that buyers who needed to form an emotional connection as part of the purchasing process were both distracted and disappointed by translation errors."

Wayne Bourland, of Dell's Global Localization Team

"In today's global economy, a thorough global linguistic evaluation is a must.

With greater access to information, more and more people can pick up on issues – and talk about them. And with greater influences from other cultures, and the rich cultural diversity of people in most countries – even when it's local, it's global.

Check names with native, in-country linguists. Idioms, slang and cultural associations vary from country to country, even if the same language is spoken. This way, you make sure your name says only what you intend it to say."

Paola Norambuena, head of verbal identity at Interbrand, the world's leading brand consultancy

Visuals are as important as words.

And even visuals designed to be international may not be as international as you think.

Corporate campaigns produced in the USA often feature mixed-gender, mixed-race working environments with whites, blacks and East Asians all represented.

But in Eastern Europe, where there has been no significant immigration from Africa and the Far East, such depictions don't reflect reality.

And in Germany, they ignore the country's largest ethnic minority – people of Turkish origin make up around 4% of the population.

Good intentions too sometimes need to be transcreated.

There's a reason why people say "Lost in translation" …

… but not "Lost in transcreation".

Maybelline's tagline "Maybe She's Born With It. Maybe It's Maybelline" works due to the repetition of the word "Maybe" and the play on words with the brand name.

But in Russian, these two linguistic techniques didn't work, so a new approach was taken:

"Все в восторге от тебя, а ты от Мэйбеллин".

This means "Everybody's enchanted by you, you're [enchanted] by Maybelline".

The omission of the second instance of "enchanted" makes the line catchy, and allows for two interpretations: "You are enchanted by Maybelline", or more subtly, "You are created by Maybelline".

It's the message of the English, but in a new, exciting form.

One of the best-selling novels of recent years is Stieg Larsson's *The Girl With The Dragon Tattoo*.

But did you know its original Swedish title, *Män Som Hatar Kvinnor,* means "Men that hate women"?

In liberal, social-democratic Sweden, the overt gender politics of the original name were no barrier to success. But the English publishers reportedly felt that a literal translation was equivalent to "Books that don't sell".

So they used a transcreation instead. And with over a million copies sold last year in the UK alone, it's hard to argue that they made the wrong decision.

When Motorola launched its new Q phone in Canada, the campaign didn't have quite the desired effect on French speakers. Unfortunately "Q" sounds like "cul" ("ass") in French.

So lines such as the ones on the opposite page raised more than a few smiles. Substitute the word "ass" for the letter "Q" and you'll see what we mean!

"Mon Q.
L'intelligence renouvelée."
("My Q. Renewed intelligence.")

"Si c'est important pour vous,
c'est important pour votre Q."
("If it's important to you,
it's important to your Q.")

Once Motorola became aware
of the mistake (the campaign
went viral shortly after
appearing on the website), it
changed it to include the full
name (Q9h).

Sometimes transcreation involves more than words.

The all-American Spider-Man comic books have been reinvented for the Indian market. The sarong-clad superhero is the alter ego of Pavitr Prabhakar (a phonetic distortion of Peter Parker), swinging from Mumbai landmarks like the Gateway of India as he fights crime in the city's teeming streets.

The character's strong family values appeal to Indian readers, and his demon-like adversaries tap into mythologies such as the Ramayana, making this a great example of how ideas can resonate across cultures.

Transcreating jingles is not just about finding the right words – they also have to fit the tune.

Gillette's German version of "The best a man can get" failed on both counts.

"Für das Beste im Mann" ("For the best inside a man") didn't really make sense – facial hair is on the outside.

Plus, the line was too short, so each word had to be dragged out longer than sounds natural.

And it doesn't even rhyme with "Gillette"!

The "Für das Be-e-e-est-e-e im Ma-a-an" jingle has therefore become something of a national laughing stock.

"Transport ... is not a good metaphor for translation, because the luggage never arrives. What interests me is what gets lost along the way."

Svetlana Geier, 1923–2010

Geier was the 20th century's pre-eminent literary translator into German, specializing in the works of Dostoyevsky. So she knew what she was talking about.

With literary works, the freer approach of transcreation may not be suitable, out of respect for the original.

But where the message is more important than the medium – as in marketing – transcreation ensures that far less is lost along the way.

So travel transcreation class, to make sure your message gets there with you.

Cost of translating
a 100-word press ad
from English into Japanese:
around £25

Cost of transcreating
a 100-word press ad
from English into Japanese:
up to £200

Ratecard for a single-page ad in
a leading Japanese paper:
£100,000

Is it worth wasting £100,000
to save around £175?

When choosing a tone, tint or hue to represent your brand, you need to think beyond how nice it will look on your marketing materials. It can mean completely different things in different cultures.

In the Western world, for example, white is associated with peace and weddings, while in Asia, white is for funerals.

In a similar vein, yellow stands for cowardice in the West, but in Japan, it means courage. And red symbolizes passion in the Western world, while in India, it means purity.

So as you can see, it's essential to do your homework before picking a shade for your international branding materials.

When the Toronto Tourist Board created an English ad advertising Christmas breaks to Toronto with the headline "Splash out" alongside a visual of waves and a visual of a fancy restaurant, they thought it was going to be impossible to make it work in French.

But by taking the creative brief and thinking outside of the box, the copywriter was able to come up with an equally appealing line that fitted with both visuals: "L'eau à la bouche", which literally translates as "water on your mouth" and means "whet your appetite" and "make someone want to do something". (In this case, visit Toronto.)

Context always matters.

Even a simple phrase like "Click to play" on a website could easily go wrong if the translator isn't properly briefed.

In most languages, the expressions "play a game" and "play a video" use different verbs.

So if you don't know what's being played, you can't translate it correctly.

Different pronunciations in different languages can be a problem – or an opportunity.

In 2009, PepsiCo found out that almost 25% of people in Argentina could not pronounce the "ps" sound. They were calling the drink "Pecsi".

Rather than fight this local idiosyncrasy, Pepsi chose to embrace it.

It ran a campaign in which
its familiar branding elements
were recreated using the
phonetic spelling.

The message was, whether
you say "Pepsi" or "Pecsi",
it still tastes better than Coke.

As a result, brand
recognition increased 23%.
Proof of what happens when
multinational brands
work with local culture.

Puns often defy translation.

This happened with a campaign for Famous Grouse whisky.

Lines like "A nice shot" (with the grouse playing golf) or "A splendid drop" (with the grouse parachuting) were literally untranslatable.

So to adapt the campaign for Greece, the brand took an enlightened approach.

Instead of saying, "We must use these lines", the agency sent the Greek copywriters a reel of 30 historic English spots, and asked them to choose four that they thought they could transcreate best.

The result was a locally relevant campaign that respected both the brand's Scottish heritage and its positioning in Greece as a young "party drink".

The TV show Fawlty Towers
has been a success all around
the world – thanks in part to
sensitive transcreation.

In the original, bumbling waiter
Manuel is a native of Barcelona.

But in the Catalan-language
version of the show that runs
on local TV in Barcelona itself,
Manuel is a Mexican.

Curiously, in the Spanish-language version of the show, the waiter is an Italian called Paolo.

Obviously Spanish state TV was hoping to export their dub to the Latin American market!

Because English is "cool", many brands decide to save the trouble of transcreating their taglines.

But even in a highly educated country like Germany (which uses a LOT of English in advertising), 2009 research found only 25% of English taglines are fully understood by 14-to-49-year-olds.

For example, cosmetics chain Douglas used the line "Come in and find out". When they realized customers understood this as "Come in and find your way out again", they had to change it to a German version.

The best way to get a message through to people is normally to give them it in their own language.

Foreign copy isn't foreign
to the people who read it.

So it shouldn't be foreign
to the people who approve it.

Any transcreation of marketing communications should always be signed off in the market where it will be used, by the relevant product manager.

The Harry Potter books have been translated into over 60 languages. But the US editions shed perhaps the most light on the transcreation process.

Famously, *Harry Potter and the Philosopher's Stone* was renamed *Harry Potter and the Sorcerer's Stone*. But the changes go deeper.

To give just one example, in the US a "jumper" is not a pullover, but a kind of dress.

By changing it to "sweater", the meaning came across in the US, but a British "feel" was retained.

The books' US publisher says. "I wasn't trying to 'Americanize' them ... I wanted to make sure that an American kid would have the same literary experience as a British kid."

This principle of recreating the reader experience is where the magic of transcreation resides.

There is more to adapting communications for foreign markets than just translating – or even transcreating – the words.

A TV spot ad for Procter & Gamble's soaps showed a man entering the bathroom while his wife was showering.

In the West, this is an entirely unremarkable scenario.

However, in Japan the husband's actions were seen as an unacceptable invasion of privacy. This seemingly innocuous ad was therefore considered to be in very poor taste.

Brands have often reached different levels of awareness, market position or advertising sophistication across different markets.

This needs to be considered when creating a new campaign based on a recognition factor.

For example, Carlsberg's "Carlsberg don't do flatmates – but if they did, they'd probably be the best flatmates in the world" TV ad relies on a knowledge of the long-running "Probably the best lager in the world" tagline. In markets where this line has not attained widespread recognition like it has in the UK, the response to the new campaign would obviously be different.

Since 1969, BMW has used the tagline "Freude am Fahren" in Germany. The English translation of this is "Pleasure in driving".

Would that be as effective as "The Ultimate Driving Machine"?

Same idea, different words —
this is what transcreation is
all about.

When creating a global ad concept, the linguistic associations that underpin it also need to be considered.

For example, a device with an exceptionally large memory might be compared to an elephant, because in the English-speaking world, elephants famously "never forget".

Equivalent comparisons probably exist in most markets. But pair the reference with an elephant visual, and it will provoke head-scratching in countries where there is no proverbial link between elephants and memory.

Transcreators are creative people. But poorly thought-out source copy risks putting this creativity in a straitjacket.

If you grew up with the Asterix books, you're already familiar with a great example of transcreation.

The characters' names are all puns, many of which don't translate – but do transcreate.

In fact, the English is sometimes even cleverer than the original French.

The names of the tone-deaf bard and food-poisoning fishmonger are merely silly in French: Assurancetourix ("assurance tous risques" means "comprehensive insurance") and Ordralfabétix ("ordre alphabétique" means "alphabetical order").

But the English names actually reflect character traits: Cacofonix for the bard, and Unhygienix for the fishmonger.

Analogies should be handled with care. What is common in one country might be inappropriate or irrelevant in another. It is therefore important to use analogies that your target market is familiar with.

Walt Disney is an excellent example of how this can be done successfully.

In the US, the Walt Disney World Resort is described as "half the size of Rhode Island". But the analogy requires some knowledge of US geography.

So in Japan, the park is said to be "the size of the Tokyo subway system", and in the UK, "the size of greater Manchester". This makes the audience feel more included – and the copy more effective.

When insurance company Aviva
created a global brand
campaign to show the
importance of their
customers, they called it
"You are the Big Picture".
This was a clever reference
to the fact that the campaign
involved customers sending in
photos of themselves to
appear on large billboard ads.
A direct translation of the
line did not have the same
effect in many languages.

The French writer transcreated the line to "L'Assurance à votre image", which literally means "Insurance in your image" and is based on an idiomatic expression: "à votre image" meaning "like you". The Polish writer, meanwhile, came up with a different photo-related play on words: "Jesteś w centrum uwagi", meaning "You're the focus of attention".

Global campaigns have two advantages compared with generating creative locally for individual markets: greater consistency of branding and messaging across markets, and reduced costs.

The risk is that they become the advertising equivalent of fast food: functional but unmemorable.

This is where transcreation comes in: it allows campaigns to walk the fine line that ensures they are both fresh and relevant locally, and at the same time consistent globally.

Idioms should be handled with caution. If translated literally, they often make little sense!

Take the English phrase "to kill two birds with one stone".

In other languages, the equivalent idioms are rather different.

Germans "hit two flies with one blow".

Chinese "shoot two hawks with one arrow".

Burmese "get two pieces with one cut".

Koreans "catch a pheasant and its eggs as well".

And Italians "snare two pigeons with one bean".

About Mother Tongue

Mother Tongue was set up in 1990 to meet the foreign-copy needs of the advertising and marketing worlds.

Our aim is to raise the standard of foreign-language marketing communications. Realizing that straight translation was often not the best option, we have evolved our services to offer our clients the most viable language solutions available.

This now includes not just copy transcreation, but also a full range of production services, including typesetting, subtitling, voice-over recording and digital, press and TV versioning.

The invaluable experience gained in these areas makes us the informed choice for anyone wishing to extend campaigns to overseas markets.

We are now used on a regular basis by many of the world's top creative agencies and marketers, because they know they can trust us to produce hard-working creative copy.

We have copywriters in all markets around the world who are skilled in the art of transcreation.

Everyone at Mother Tongue is passionate about what we do. We are all committed to producing top-quality copy for foreign markets that is as powerful and effective as the original.

Transcreation
Ad versioning
Foreign voice-over
Production services
Concept research
Subtitling